City Life

City Life

poems

FREDERICK FEIRSTEIN

Story Line Press | *Pasadena, CA*

City life

ISBN 978-1-58654-074-6 (tradepaper)
      978-1-58654-089-0 (casebound)

The National Endowment for the Arts, the Los Angeles County Arts Commission, the
Ahmanson Foundation, the Dwight Stuart Youth Fund, the Max Factor Family Foun-
dation, the Pasadena Tournament of Roses Foundation, the Pasadena Arts & Culture
Commission and the City of Pasadena Cultural Affairs Division, the City of Los Ange-
les Department of Cultural Affairs, the Audrey & Sydney Irmas Charitable Foundation,
the Kinder Morgan Foundation, the Meta & George Rosenberg Foundation, the Aller-
gan Foundation, the Riordan Foundation, Amazon Literary Partnership, and the Mara
W. Breech Foundation partially support Red Hen Press.

Second Edition
Published by Story Line Press
an imprint of Red Hen Press
www.redhen.org

Acknowledgments

The poet wishes to thank the John Simon Guggenheim Memorial Foundation
for their grant which gave him time to work on this book.

Acknowledgments are made to the magazines in which these poems first appeared:

Denver Quarterly:"Bag Lady Lullaby"; *The Kenyon Review:*"The Abortion," "The
Eyes"; *The Nation:* "Father and Son"; *The Ontario Review:* "Divorced," "The Grand-
son," "Belle's Café", "Purple Hearts," (originally called "The Old Neighborhood");
Present Tense:"The Boarder" (also in *Survivors*); *Salmagundi:*"Siddhartha Dove."

Poems from the dramatic sequence "The Psychiatrist At The Cocktail Party"
have appeared in *The Ontario Review*, *Pulpsmith*, *The Reaper*, and the
anthology *Light Year*.

In memory of Roger Hecht

CONTENTS

City Life

LARRY'S NEIGHBORHOOD

THE ABORTION

When they met her hands could cradle a fish.
She could pluck his smallest hurts
Like barnacles from a baby's face.
And when he betrayed her with a woman
Twice her age and a boy half, she would hold
Her breath like a diver looking for pearls.
And when she was a girl, she would sit
On her alcoholic mother's lap and pick
Loose threads from her slip. Oh,
Life is a sinker, Death a threaded worm,
Her mother's wriggling finger, making her squirm.
One must be as the fisherman Christ,
One must weave a net of solitary days:
The pressed dress waiting on the bed,
The doorbell untouched as her nipples,
The windows changing seasons like slides,
The fish tank furiously reproducing,
The neighbors' merciless undisciplined kids,
The traffic of funerals underneath her fire escape,
The hysterectomy underneath her pants,
The bitten fingernails and the feet too pigeon-toed to dance.
But the shark has bitten the net and bloodied her wrist.
She runs the twisted bed sheet between her legs
And can't understand why he not she is allowed to exist.
She's forgotten exactly the means of his crime.
She can't recall his idiosyncrasies, even his name.
But she knows there's a fishy smell in this room,
And she began a note, though she's crumpled it where?
She wrote, "I'm no longer angry, I'm no longer sad.
I've just had it, I've honestly had."

DIVORCED

His walls are soiled with his children's handprints.
His bed is chronically unmade.
He can't cook, eats junk food standing up,
Has no will to go out and get laid

But has wet dreams on his wife's pillow,
Job applications slide off his best chair
—Colonial American, its frame
Disjointed, warped beyond repair.

His father who would worship him is dead.
His mother, once his closest friend,
Mistakes him for her nurse when she's alert.
He's greedy for whatever she pretends.

His wife gave plants excessive care,
When he quit his job, smeared his face with dirt.
His children were aloof. He thought they'd feel
Insecure, as least, when they saw him hurt.

His apartment building is a D.P. camp,
The street below a road for refugees
Carrying loads too much for innocents
To bear. She said she needed to be free,

Had spent her best years watching t.v. soaps,
Yet blamed him (Pig!) for her own lack
Of nerve. Each night, a boy, he kneels
Beside their bed, praying she will come back.

He spent the first months trying to visit friends.
All of them were booked with business dates,
All spoke in neutral operator tones
Or, when he wept, tried to simulate

Analytic silence. What will he do
To fill Time's empty gift boxes? Smoke
His fingers brown, walk out at midnight
Hoping to get mugged, snort coke?

THE SHAWL

1. SIDDHARTHA DOVE

We screw, then you lecture me on "The East"
Because you say my better half is black,
Then mock that white gal's photo on my desk:
That was my wife. That was no playful smack
Across your ass. Don't say, "Listen at least!"

My daughter also had contempt for whites.
She called herself "Historically deprived."
She missed out on The War and Civil Rights.
She developed that same missionary smile
Toward me—"decadent for having thrived

In a Western meditative racket." Her eyes
Crossed when I said, "Do ghetto social work,"
As a 1940s starlet might've looked
At the proposal of a soda jerk.
My training taught me never to advise

Anyone. Mulattoes never know their place.
This was her room, usually a mess.
She tried to sketch her idols: Chairman Mao,
Like you she loved "poor Che"—and Herman Hesse.
Some politics! That's her baby-face

The day she turned into Siddhartha Dove.
Her Deide doll, her bike, her leather thongs,
Her button from the rally for Reverend Moon.
That hair's her relic ... "What radical's?" King Kong's!
Her great-great grandmother's face: an octoroon

Runaway—a genuine Matthew Brady.
She married and became an English lady
And moved to India. Resemblance strange?
Her water pipe . . . My wife was dead, I did my best!
That pain, not Hesse, sent her on her "quest."

She painted my army knapsack baby-pink.
She painted her t-shirt with her guru's face.
She painted a red dot on her forehead.
"This country doesn't give me growing space,"
She said. "A shrink's daughter doesn't shrink

From exploration." Her No Smoking sign.
I bought it, angry at her innocence:
"You will not find pollution in Bombay."
She sent me this sealed vial for evidence,
To sniff the air around her guru's shrine.

After a while: months between her notes—
"Afghanistanis shower me with dope . . .
I had a child, I sold him, that's okay . . .
Don't worry, I won't try the snake and rope.
I got a gig this summer herding goats."

She died in bed, a Delhi gutter, cut
More often than a Christian saint.
Her begging cup ran over with her blood.
A Third World proselytizer shouldn't faint!
A begging gang had sewn her mild mouth shut,

A lesson for the other Hesse kids.
Never again would she eat their precious trash.
Never again compete for *Baksheesh* (alms).
In scorn they blacked her dying face with ash.
None had the Western grace to close her lids . . .

No, stay. I want your company tonight.
I hate your politics, but I love your sex . . .
You'll need to joke when you're my age . . . I'll make
You give up Arabs? Keep your arabesques
And move a little closer to the right.

2. THE EYES

A colored psychoanalyst?
Sorry. You want me to sit here?
You look half-Jewish. My wife's friend
Belle *nudged* me to come. I hope
You're not a Muslim. Do you have
A son? Sorry. "Why?"
I can see pain in your eyes
—My field is ophthalmology,
Or was. I'm not retired, but
I can't work. I guess that's why I've come . . .

I joined a *shul* to give my son a home
After I died—with nostalgic smells:
Satin and parchment. Who believed
The Auschwitz God could hear a prayer?
Him!: "When the black plague destroyed
Half Europe's Christians, they fell to their knees

And found cause in their own lack
Of faith." I wanted to stop there
—The satin, the parchment. My wife
Ignored me, dug out her mother's shawl
And *bentsht lichtn* each Friday night.
And we had *seders* every spring,
And sang in grass Quonset huts
On Sukkos, and wept Kol Nidre nights . . .

You want to hear "a dream?" My son
Drifts from heaven in a parachute
Dawning, a baby in a swing,
At eighteen pretty as his mother,
Eyes the color of Israel's flag.
SUNSET IN LEBANON—A Dream
With Titles Or, A Dream With Guns!
I mock analysis as I do
All faiths because, because my son . . .
They brought him back from *Yisroel*
With heaven where his eyes were!

Back to "the problem," why I've come:
At 6 A.M. I leave for *shul*
With my bad heart, trudging
Through drifts of snow.
I, not my son, say *Kaddish.*
I sit with my forehead
Pressed on the bench in front of me
Till *Maariv* when I snap
To attention and mumble more . . .
You seem to know what *Maariv* is
—All these Yiddishisms.

There's something in your eyes. Are you
A *Falasha*? Something kindred . . .

So I sit like a Talmudist
In *shul* all day
Eating a sandwich from a paper bag
Or curled up, snoring, till the sun sets
—And then it's up like a believer
Waiting for *Kaddish* in the evening prayers . . .
But if I don't endure these rituals,
How will he find me
When I come to Heaven,
A blur, a shadow
Blabbering because his wife—and Belle—
Are worried for his heart,
A wife who *bentshes lictn* still,
His picture like a saint's
In front of her except, except he's draped
In that same shawl—that flag
In which we buried him!

YIDDISHISMS, etc.

      nudge - pestered
      shul - synagogue
      bensht lichtin - blessed (the Sabbath) candles
      seders - Passover meals
      Sukkos - Harvest Festival
      Kol Nidre - prayer of atonement
      davning - praying
      Yisroel - Israel
      Kaddish - prayer for the dead
      Maariv - the evening service

      Falasha - Ethiopian Jew

Excuse me, but your eyes seem blurred.
Has my story moved you,
Or have you heartache from a son?
You won't say . . . Silence . . . Where am I going?
I can get the same from *Kaddish*.
That picture on your desk, is she
Your daughter, draped in a sari,
Red dot on her forehead, eyes fogged
With that same religious look?
A nod. I need a friend to share
My tragedy, and you have your technique.
I'm sorry. When you see Belle,
Please tell her not to worry. She's blessed
With a pregnant daughter and a selfish son.

3. BELLE'S CAFÉ

The census-taker? Show me proof. Come in.
Excuse my bathrobe. Sit. Didn't I mail
My form to you? I thought I filled it in.
I don't have much to offer, just a cup
Of tea, maybe a piece of mandlebread.
They used to call my kitchen "Belle's Café"
And fed me with their troubles while they ate . . .
It's nicer, yes? to sit and work this way.
You write. The medication makes me shake.
See how this tea cup rattles? Don't write *that*!
"Stone" was my maiden name. My husband's dead.
Over a year ago. In May. I've got
One daughter and a grandson and a son.
Excuse me but sometimes it helps to pace.

No, don't come back tomorrow. I can talk.
In fact, if it's a good day, I might take
A walk to the market with my friend. She
Has troubles! Yet *she* is a citizen.
Her husband is incapable of work.
An atheist, he sits in shul all day
And I can't sit for thirty seconds straight!
My therapist, who tries with me, will spout,
"We move between the poles of love and hate,
Trying to merge, trying to separate."
So, where's my household?—Question 5—The grave!
I'm sorry. You're a stranger and, in spite
Of all the help I get, I can't
Be brave. Not like my friend who lost her son.
I'm not a person but a part of one.
When my husband died, I didn't cry, not once
And we did everything together, talked
On the phone a dozen times a day, slept
Together, shopped together, and when he drove
I spouted the directions. Now I've none.
And so put down for Question 6: a half
A person lives at 20-55,
Dressed in a bathrobe, boring a stranger,
Pacing to show that half is still alive!
I'm sorry for these outbursts. You've just come
To take the facts. You're probably not the type
Who even wants to know what made a life
Statistical. That's why you've chosen this work.
But for the future, take my case to heart:
Those who live too close or far apart
From others are the same. One can't survive
Alone. The other seriously doubts

That he's alive. I'm like your mother, right?
And you're like mine—and also like my son
Who works as an accountant, and who calls
Me, even in this state, "The Know-It-All,"
And visits, if I'm lucky, once a month,
And lets me tell my troubles to his wife
By phone! And now it's time for you to go
And time for me to rest before I pace
—Between love for my husband and hate,
Trying to merge, trying to separate.

4. THE GRANDSON

"Me reweth, Marye, thy sone and thee"
("SUNSET IN CALVARY")

I'm not a pretty woman, never was.
My nose is surgically small, my eyes slitty.
My hair, even when combed, looks electrified.
My legs, poor things, are like a pelican's.
But men have always like my being witty,
Especially my soldier—he was young,
Talkative, generous, blond, blue-eyed
—His eyes were cowish, a shade of dung!
I overstepped myself again—no tact.
This room is sheltered, quiet, don't you think?
A bed that cranks up like an ak-ak gun,
A vase of exploding roses.
Shutup shutup shutup shutup.
Are you a male nurse, social worker, shrink?
—Angelic in white, a beard like Moses.

A pelican's some symbol for a Jew.
And the good doctors of Jerusalem
Cut the cord from his neck, turning him pink.
What's that gurgling, bubbling in the sink?
Nothing. Petals folding like two hands in prayer.
My soldier was 19. I am 31.
Homesick New Yorkers making *Aliyah*.
We made love one night, one night, that's all.
Enough to start the deadly birth: the Fall
Of Isaac was his name—appropriate?
Ten pounds of scrunchy fat and smiles,
And talkative? He wouldn't shutup.
Some nights I told him I'd mute him—he'd smile.
Some nights I told him I'd give him away,
He was driving me crazy—no sleep—he'd smile.
Baby, I'd say, I've got a delicate *kup*
With fantasies, shmantasies driving me wild.
I'd sing to him, Go to sleep, drop dead, my child.
Cut to a kibbutz, rest cure, no street
Noises, no cars, cabs, buses, trucks.
Smash a champagne bottle against the sky—
Stars! Carve a piece of feta cheese—moon!
And blessed exhaustion after a mute day's work.
And how I loved to see him in the mornings
Kick at his mobile, blue-eyed. Were his father's dung?
Oh he was handsome, what's-his-name, and young.
Alarms, alarms, snatch babies out of their cribs,
Running across courtyard, down to the shelter
Shutup shutup shutup shutup:
The terrorists are really coming,
Triggers of Kalashnikovs they're strumming,
And I am rocking him to sleep and humming.

But shutup shutup *Sha! They'll kill us all,*
Unless you quiet him! I take my shawl
And wrap it like a shroud around his face.
His eyes are frantic—shh—a second more.
I hear them, don't you, running past the door?
Why doesn't he answer me—Yitzhak?
Isaac? Shmendrik? Aren't I witty?
They never told me I'd be pretty.
But I've become a tragic heroine.
I'm praised and mourned in all of the cafés.
Are you an angel glowing there in white,
Or am I doped by all these pills I've taken?
Green ones, yellow ones, purple ones, pink.
I know I should get up and vomit in the sink
Or stand inside a shower leaking gas.
I'll lie beside my baby, and the grass
Will cover us brown as dung, and when the birds
Try to waken us for the Apocalypse,
We'll whisper to them, both in baby-talk,
Shutup shutup shutup shutup.

THE BOARDER

Stubborn Spring pushed through the cold twigs
In the small park across the street
From where Yud Schwartz, the poet, lived
With a deaf butcher and the butcher's wife
In one room cluttered as his grief:
Pictures of his dead wife on his desk
And of Schwartz, Sholem Aleichem and Sholem Asch—
Three cypresses on a Bronx street,
Two of them dead, Yud Schwartz
Cut down as well. His bookcase was
A crypt; his Yiddish tongue was dust;
And she dead a week—
Ruts for the skidding wheels of a Ford.

 "How do I feel? I woke at dawn
  In a yellow sweat, my sheets wet,
  My guts wood, my head stuffed with grass,
  With bluebird bones, fragments of poems.
  I dressed. Buttoning my shirt was hard,
  Believe me. 'There's one choice,' I said.
  'Make up your mind!' and I half-walked
  Down to the part. Forty-six steps—
  I counted every one of them.
  The clouds were rinsed of simile,
  The sky bluer than Galilee.
  The buds were out. I touched them: frail
  As a wren's tongue, pale. The earth felt
  Like bear's fur. Good, damn it, it's good.

 "How do I feel?" He read a poem:
  About wind, papers wrapped tight on his calves
  As he walked Sholem Aleichem's streets, the old shops

Gone, slush soaking his shoes—gone poor,
Spanish in the tenement rooms
Where he spent the Sabbath afternoons
With his young wife, his poet-friends,
Peeled yellow apples and munched nuts,
Munched figs, and vowed to eat the world.

In fall I telephoned. "Who?" said the butcher's wife.
"The poet." "Who?" "The boarder!" "Dead.
Last Spring. He left no money and no clothes."

FATHER AND SON

Awkward, the winter whirling behind us
Through monolithic towers of glass,
Not through medieval woods where your death
Is private and unbearable, we wait.
I want to hold your hand, and yet you walk
Away, the snow spotting your face, your hair,
Back through the drifts quaintly, forcing a show
Of courage, when I want to speak once more.
What do we do with death in this cold age,
When neglect piles bodies up like worn-out tires,
When . . . ? Suddenly a clock strikes *Now*.
My hand twitches like a tuning fork.
I expect a horseman in a black mask
To gallop down the avenue and snatch me up.
Not you, because I'm still a child and you
Must whip him off, not stoop into a cab
Whose whitening windows slowly lose your face.

BAG LADY LULLABY

An orphan's Christmas in Central Park.
Delacorte's clock plays a lullaby
Only for Christ's sake and the stranded birds.
The trees, toy soldiers, stand poised in ice.
The snow unnoticed practices pirouettes.
The wind, an infant's father, holds its breath.
But a bag lady in a loud red
And blue blanket crashes in: "Soup's on!"
She announces to the abandoned park.
"Your Momma's back. Not like mine,
Thank God! . . . Is anyone still alive?"
She sings. "Ruffle your feathers for a sign."
She tut tuts and mock-weeps.
She pulls her sleeves up like a magician
And reaches deep in her bag for a loaf
Of black bread. "Momma ever forget you?"
She freckles her feet, her knees, her thighs,
Her belly, her breasts, wrists, shoulders, head
With "Bread! Bread! Bread!" and sits stone still.
As on Christmas Day the rich widows,
Dressed as kings brought gifts to The Home.

HOME

He loiters in the doorway—a bruise-red face,
A green pint of wine in his coat pocket,
Round as a punching bag, wobbly from too much deference,
I tell him, "I know it's cold but this urine stinks."
He moves his head like a grandma from side to side.
He pats the wall as if it's a baby's face.
"I used to be a bricklayer. I still
Remember building this, good and strong."
He closes his eyes and, humming a lullaby,
Presses his forehead against the intercom.
"Stay," I say. "Warm yourself for a few minutes,
Then please go." *The old women who live here*
Will be frightened. They can't recognize
Anyones's helplessness but their own.
I'm afraid you'll shit on the tiles
Or lurch accidentally against my pregnant wife.
I say none of these things, only smile.
"You're a real old-fashioned guy," he winks.
"If everyone was a little more like you, I would try."
I want to tell him: *This lobby*
Is half its old size, the landlord
Tore its walls down to make a porno bookstore.
I can understand the logic of your degradation
And could speak intimately of my sorrows
If you wouldn't nod at them like another lie.
"I'll go soon," he reassures me, as I turn my key
In the forbidden door. I look back to see
He doesn't follow me in. He understands my mistrust
And smiles as if I've kicked him in the belly.
"Take care of yourself," I say, as if he could.
"This was a better world once," he says. "Goodbye."

PURPLE HEARTS

He wore that woolen shirt for thirty years.
The same? His cronies wouldn't doubt it.
And those corrective shoes flecked with blood,
The soles worn thin as wafers,
And those suspenders dangling from his neck?
The same. Nothing changed him, not four muggings,
Not permanently. Watch: His knuckles nailed
Against the floor will clench, and he'll rise
A fighter to his knees, Get up, Charley!
And his eyes will roll back down and blink.
Get up, Charley! and he'll say, "A man endures,"
And show his bruises off like Purple Hearts.

Outside the political clubs, on orange crates
Or on their brownstones' stoops, the old men talk,
Swap Charley stories, obituaries
Of their neighborhood, a small town
In the grip of junkies . . .
One fingers his throat where Charley choked.
One kisses his hand and touches the air.
One jabs his hearing aid at vacant heaven.
One plugs his ears and hums.

In dime-store Westerns they learned English from,
Someone tall, not stooped by stroke like Charley,
Stubbornly stayed in town, his door unlatched,
His goods donations to the elderly.
Bad guys shot up his store for fun, bottles
For practice. Charley's a broken bottle.
"At least he got his pictures in the papers."
"Yeah, but who could see his face?" "They saw

His name. They'd recognize his woolen shirt."
So the doomed talk into the concrete night.
If no one takes the chance to mug them, time will.

THE PSYCHIATRIST
AT THE COCKTAIL PARTY

A DRAMATIC POEM

CHARACTERS

Ben Struthers—the psychiatrist
Larry—the host of the cocktail party
Bea—Larry's mother
Joyce—Larry's fiancée
Steve—Joyce's son

Renee—Larry's friend from college
"Meato"—owner of meat markets, Renee's husband
Renee's Dance Partner

The Guest Of Honor, Juarez—a rebel leader from
Quistador
The Right Hand, Jimenez—The Guest Of Honor's
second in command

The Old Maid
Joe—a "headhunter"
Mark Stern—owner of a business selling New York
City souvenirs

LARRY CORNERS THE PSYCHIATRIST

Look who's standing in my bedroom door!
Give me your coat, Ben. Glad you could come
To one of my fund-raising bashes.
This one is for that man from Quistador.
Startling, these guys in khaki and mustaches.
Try an hors d'oeuvre. The catering is yum.

Where's Mary? . . . Jeez, does she have a fever?
I hope it's just the flu and nothing more.
Even you'd be a hypochondriac
With my mother—it was so hard to leave her.
I wish Mary wasn't flat on her back;
I wanted her to see my new décor.

It's Pop-Colonial, a parody:
Brighton bamboo, but painted Third World red.
The knicknacks are from 42nd Street,
Las Vegas, and Disneyland: *our* ivory
But crafted out of plastic—Go on, eat—
And not one single elephant shot dead.

Mary would have loved our rebel guest,
An illustration of her Ph.D.
On Latin intellectuals *cum* killer.
I think this baby far outstrips the rest.
He has a Harvard social work degree
And still reads shrink books. God, I think he'd thrill her.

The women love him, so he said to Joyce
Jokingly. Doc, while I still have your ear,
I want to tell you something. Please don't smirk.
I think I may be making the wrong choice

In getting married. (Hi, Steve.) Come stand here.
Each time I get engaged, my goddamn quirk

Obsesses me—is that the proper word?
Some aspect of her body starts to look
—Her breasts, her neck, even the way she walks—
Like Mom's or Sis's. Isn't that absurd?
I've haunted bookstores, looking for a book
About this. You know my shrink never talks

But simply nods or says, "In time we'll see."
Except that lately I can't get it up!
When Joyce lies on her side, her torso's curve
Is Mom's! I know what you must think of me.
Our little Larry got a crazy kup.
Our little Shmedipus ain't got the nerve,

I hear my coffee magnate father say,
That's why I left a trust fund for the jerk.
He can't support himself in love or work.
That's not the truth. You want to hear it, Ben?
You want to hear the only, maddening way
A woman makes my soldier stiffen?

Remember when I first came on to Joyce?
—Before her husband died, when she was his.
Exactly when I first came on to Liz,
Nancy, and Beth. All mothers of a boy
Rebellious as I was! I should keep my voice
Down. Can you hear me? I hope this won't destroy

Our friendship, Ben. Don't smile. I'm serious.
Joyce was your student, sort of like your child.

You see Renee dancing? It drives me wild
To watch her luring her husband. It
Makes me absolutely delirious.
I think deep down I can't leave Momma's tit.

I'm boring you, you hear this every day
And write that sex is often infantile.
I will not toddle down the wedding aisle,
Hoping that once your Joyce becomes my wife
This craziness will somehow go away,
And that at forty-two I'll change my life!

Please think about this as you mingle here.
Joyce shouldn't have to tough this out with me,
Her husband dead. I bet her son is gay.
I wonder if I have a buried fear
Of "hamasexuality," as Dad would say.
I can't believe that I am fidgety

Around Renee, and that the Meat King
Her husband—that fat, that ignorant, that crass
Wholesale butcher is what I really crave,
That somewhere in me I am conjuring
His slipping a long bratwurst up my ass.
I am my mother's not my father's slave!

I was attracted to Renee in school,
Before the Meat King crawled into her bed.
But then I wasn't rich enough, an heir;
Just a Momma's boy, a cheerleader, a fool.
But now, however, I am debonair,
A boy to flirt with, now that my father's dead.

TO LARRY WHO DOUBTS HE SHOULD MARRY

Larry, imagine after dying that your soul
Wakes up in a barren, rural home
In Quistador—genetically a gnome,
But smart, aware of living in a hole

From watching t.v., watching men like you
Throw parties where they somberly confess
They feel powerless when they undress,
Or get excited by some rebel's coup.

Imagine *being* like you're feeling, Larry,
And think concretely of your peasants' lives,
The helplessness they suffer with their wives,
And how they'd laugh to hear you might not marry

Because you're too "obsessed" to make a home
With Joyce who gives you what you'd rather give
Politically—to strangers. Larry, live
As if you're not inhabiting a gnome.

All day I hear my patients curse their fate,
How psychologically they re-create
Their parents tyrannizing them with guilt
Until their penises refuse to tilt,
How history seems passed down in their genes:
Oedipus zipping down his gabardines

And, like you, finding Guess who? Mother!
Abel getting all A's, despite his brother
Who beats him nightly when the lights are out,
And wakes up in adulthood wracked by doubt.
I don't speak glibly when I say rejoice,
Suffer your neurosis. But marry Joyce.

LARRY'S MOTHER

You're Doctor Struthers, aren't you?
The former mentor of his fiancée
I'm Larry's mother. Call me Bea.
Larry never thinks of introducing me,
As if he's lying and I might give him away,
Or set up an intriguing rendezvous.

Though Larry's Harvard, I am crass
And all his friends find me refreshing. So,
What do you think? You like the merchandise?
You're puzzled, but you giggled twice.
Am I a psychiatric type that you don't know,
Or just an agèd piece of ass?

I was a Catskill comedienne.
True. Always "on," always playing a part
Till Larry's father, may he rest in peace,
Insisted on calling me, not Bea, but Beatrice,
And that I had more than a mouthpiece—a heart.
That isn't cockamamie, Ben.

If I might be presumptuous
(Who me?), I'd like to solicit
(Please no blushing, no erection)
Your thoughts about this insurrection
Larry's supporting now in Quistador. No thoughts on it?
Try the stuffed shrimp: they're scrumptious.

Tell me if this is self-destructive: Quistador
Borders the country where we import
Our coffee beans. Larry says
To me, only to me, Juarez

Will leave our crops alone if we support
His cause, if we serve schnapps to the señor.

But now, of course, I overhear my Larry
Talk only of ideals to everyone.
Did he reveal this other side to you?
He's not your patient, there is no taboo
Involved. Believe me, it ain't fun
To ask you. Your pet Joyce he plans to marry

Don't know, or else won't say. That shrimp is good.
The caterer was my lover. So,
Knowing Larry, what do you think?
What will you have to drink?
Take your time, but tell me what you know.
Our coffee business now is thriving, knock on wood.

But if it goes, and I am gone,
What happens to my son? How will he fend
For himself—he's never done it—on his wits?
Under pressure Larry quits.
You know how as a kid he used to defend
Himself in school? He'd befriend the scum,

Or give them money so they wouldn't beat him up.
Like now—I never thought of it!
You see what happens even talking to a shrink?
Your golden silence made me think!
He's buying protection, the little shit.
Let me pour *our* coffee in your cup.

JOYCE

Hello, Doctor . . . Why am I looking glum?
I didn't realize, Ben. Show me the look.
I'm glad that you could leave your work and come . . .
See patients on a Saturday? Silly,
I thought you might be working on your book!
Where's Mary? I hope she isn't ill. She
Doesn't take much care of your . . . her body. Larry
Is somewhere back there asking someone if
He finally ought to take the plunge and marry.
What do I want to do? Pour me a stiff
Drink and I'll tell you. Sometimes, Mine Herr Shrink
—Always—I want to run away in time
And be your fawning student, whoops! I think
There's more than scotch and soda in this. I'm
Getting high on talking to you. I hate
Larry's parties for these dwarfs of history
Like that one with the beard, that second-rate
Castro with his obligatory bad-
Mouthing America. Here's my son.

. . .

You know Dr. Struthers. How's the party, Steve?
I'm glad you like the Guest of Honor. He
(Larry claims) will soon take over Quistador
And bring equality to everyone.
Larry's raising money for his war.
Yes, try your Spanish out on him. I'm glad
You're interested. But tell me when you leave.

. . .

What is he doing? Just driving me mad.
But I don't want to talk about Steve yet.
The music's playing, and I want to dance.
I want to close my eyes and fantasize
That I'm in college with the power to
(Don't laugh) destroy your analytic stance.
That's what I thought when I looked up at you
This way, knowing of course you liked the look.
I knew because you'd either rub your eyes
Or look for something (safety?) in your book,
Or ask me questions like you're doing now.
I haven't laughed all week. *Stop, Joyce. Ask him how
His patients are.* How's Mary? Glad she's healthy,
And Larry's well, and Larry's very wealthy.

RENEE'S HUSBAND

I'd like to introduce you to my wife
Who's in the powder room. Her name's Renee.
She's beautiful but needs to live in strife
—Only with me, a charitable man.
Doctor, would you snitch a canapé
For me, by reaching over if you can?

Why should I suffer? When I was a child
My mother would always battle
Not with my father, not with my brother—*me*,
Though I never acted wild.
She'd holler when I'd shake my rattle,
Or suddenly shake me violently.

But I want to get back to my wife,
Doctor. As you'll see when you see her mood
Swings, swinging from bad to good,
She gives me no calm in my life
Which I need with a mother like that.
Do we choose our mates from the past,
Looking for love that can't last?
She's like an acrobat

Not in bed, but with emotions.
I want her on medication
—True Women's Liberation
From all her crazy notions
Of how I'm black and white, of how I
Deprive her, showering her with gifts.
She yells it is for *me* I give her little lifts,
And why don't I let her die?

• • •

Renee, come meet this fine psychiatrist.
I didn't catch your name at first.
Put that drink down. I insist.
Have a coke if you're "dying of thirst!"
These canapés are great. Aren't they Doc?
Not gin and tonic! Tell her it's no good,
On top of these ups for her mood,
To drink, that they'll put her into shock.
What she buys from these dealers is *shlock!*
It's better she mix food:
Liverwurst, frankfurters . . . Would
You bite them like you bite my cock!
What do you mean? He's used
To hearing words like this!
Tell him how you bite when we kiss,
When you're getting, like now, juiced.

• • •

Please, Doc, don't wander off.
I know you don't like talking,
You guys—silent types who cough
Ahem, ahem. Don't start walking
Away from me, or else I'll give you you-know-what.
Don't stare like her who's cool.
Especially when I'm hot.
Don't treat me like an infantile fool
Who, when he's rattled, will shake.
I'm not the kind of man
Who'd rather bend than break

But will do everything he can.
Why am I talking like this,
When I'm asking for your assistance
To help my wife, not piss
You off with what she calls my butcher's persistence?

So here I've introduced you to my wife
Who's eating like she should to keep her health.
We'd like a consultation. Please, your card.
The fee's no matter. I'm a man of wealth
Who'll pay what's necessary iill this strife
Between us ends. You'll be her bodyguard
Because one day I'll go, I'm scared,
Out of control, if she keeps acting mad
At me, at what's inside her, at the wall
She always bangs when we're embattled,
When I act cool, when I call her on all
Her manipulations, when I refuse to get rattled.

• • •

Put that drink down. Where are you going?
A mood swinging her to that good-looking man.
Dance with him, bitch. Stand up if you can.
Do you see how she's showing
You, spitefully, how nuts she can be,
Deserting me like this,
Giving that stranger a kiss?
Look at what she does to me!

RENEE'S DANCE PARTNER

Look at that Spanish guy in camouflage,
Those Calvin Klein fatigues and combat boots,
That beard trimmed in a mirror in the woods
Where Larry sends him whiskey and canned goods,
Like Larry's father stocked an Elks Club lodge
With little franks and long cheroots.
Why these phallic images, Doc?
Why am I fighting down an urge to tweak
A chin hair from that strutting, radically chic
Cartoon? Let's do, "She loves me, loves me not"
On him, sprinkle this caviar with snot,
These slices of—what's this?—our Larry's cock?
You should have listened to the malice of
That quasi-nymphomaniac Renee,
The one whose husband riveted your ear.
She told me if you treated her, she'd play
With you with words; then when you fell in love
With her, she'd screw you to the wall with fear
Of suicide, malpractice, homicide
—Until I felt it bulging in my pants.
Isn't that weird? She knew, giggled,
Urged everyone to watch me dance.
I parodied a Charleston, till I wiggled
Into the bathroom where I jerked it down,
Thinking of Larry's girlfriend. Listen, Joyce
Is not the girl for him. She's smart, she's kind,
The only woman in this phony town
I ever loved, could love. And who's her choice
To give her inner riches to, to marry?
This 1960s throwback, little Larry.

I'll tell you now what's cooking in my mind,
And brings these little franks and Larry's cock
Together. Larry (You'll think this nuts)
In college had the hots for guess who? Crazy
Renee, the pom pom Queen, whose every honey
Was someone with a hoard of family money,
Like him the Meat King with his chopped meat putz.
Not sentimental Larry she called "lazy."
We'll dance again. But this time when we kiss,
Slipping a pill from mouth to mouth, I think
I'll tell her—leading her by the waist outside—
That the way to zap her husband for the shrink-
Sending he wants to do is to piss
Him off right now by taking Larry for a ride
In Meato's big back-seated Rolls (Un!) Royce
While I, in the commotion, comfort Joyce.

THE OLD MAID

You're flirting with me, though I'm half-alive,
Trapped in a body turning forty-five.
I made those lines up, Doctor, like a guy,
Not to flirt, but to subtly ask you why
I'm at this party for this silly cause
When everyone I've met here so far bores
Me with their chatter, while their heads turn back
At every sexy twenty-year-old snack.
What would you call them: Children? Pederasts?
Afraid of Time? Of anything that lasts?
I've put my years in on the couch (not bed),
Trying to leave a world inside my head
Of Family, Neighborhood—all crazy, yet
Much warmer than this world, this silhouette
Of business people, using work instead
Of family for a place to block their dread
Of isolation, like this party for
That Latin Marxist, womanizing bore.
What do you think his politics could be
When he's pinched each woman on the ass but me,
Only because I never turned my back
To him? These macho guys are gay, attack
The ass, afraid of what a woman can
Present. Deep down, I think, they want a man.
That's what this party's for—to celebrate
The revolution of that potentate
Over his constitution—which is gay.
Look at the way he mouths his canapé
While talking to that boy—is that Joyce's son?—
About artillery, the kind of fun
You have as they recoil and make a hole
To burrow in like some sex-crazy mole.

Is this what men don't want in me, my wit?
My realistic view of life? My grit?
There's nothing wrong with me except my age,
Our age we live in like our body's cage.
Doctor, if there were world enough and time,
We'd have no tragedies, no walls to climb.

. . .

What do I think of your guest, that Latin lover?
With good analysis, he might recover
The early motives of his need to kill.
No joke. I think he's seriously ill,
As everyone who makes not love, but war.
Without his jargon? Just a Conquistador.
Sorry you asked me? No? Then, listen, Larry.
Throw the next party for when you marry
Joyce, or for life, at least for food relief,
Not for this creep who brings us death and grief.
You know, you're also nearly forty-five.
It is miraculous to be alive
—Lonely or crazy, poor, rich, middle-class—
Wanting a piece of male or female ass,
Not this destroyer in his khaki slime,
This bore, this thief of other people's time.

. . .

What do you think of Larry? Should I ask?
Failed in some developmental task?
Maybe of separating from his mother,
So that he has a need to undercover

Merge with a stronger man to help him leave
The safety of her skirts? Am I naïve
In using psychoanalytic jargon? No!
I like your laugh, Doctor. Shall we gossip at
Each fool we see? Or would you rather chat
With someone younger, sexier? No crime
To want a newer packaging of Time.
You hear the way I deprecate myself,
A dusty bottle on a dusty shelf?
Empty except when I am feeling witty.
Beneath these battle scars, you know, I'm pretty.
Dust me off, I'll turn into a genie.
I used to call my analyst a meanie
When he looked trapped like that. And he was right.
I've got to run. Have a good time tonight.

THE GUEST OF HONOR

Of course I know Dr. Struthers! Author of
Father and Sons, Macho Men/Their Mothers,
Two of the books I take into the hills
To teach my people how to bring out love
In what we call our sisters and our brothers.
I read aloud as we go through drills.

You look amused. Bewildered. Tell me what!
Señor, this isn't flattery. It's fact.
I've even read your esoterica,
Under a palm tree on an army cot
—That one on how we're doomed to re-enact
(All of us, not just the hysteric) "The

Death of Mirroring Self-Objects." Have you read
McPhee's provocative biography? No?
His thesis is I'm driven to repeat
My father's being pummeled in his bed.
Each strategy repeats each murderous blow
Struck by his first son, adopted from the street!

Intriguing? Shall I stay in New York City,
On your couch, and put my actions into words,
With no assassin in the waiting room,
Until we find the psychic nitty-gritty?
—As doctors used to look in their kings' turds
For signs of self-destructiveness and doom.

Sorry for being light. McPhee cuts deep.
Down there you're taught to treat your wounds with action;
Food, food and more food when they sense my state
—Despair!—when they can't wake me up from sleep.
There's developing a Young Turk faction
Ready to destroy me—full of hate,

Full of macho turds to fill their emptiness,
Their empty mothers that they've got inside,
Frightened child-women who abandoned them,
Like mine . . . It's not too difficult to guess
The way she acted when my father died.
A son was something merely to condemn

Like the judge condemned my brother. She'd look
For signs of violence, madness in me, though
I was her own, though I had different genes.
I had to keep my nose pressed to a book.
If I was struck, I couldn't strike a blow.
The schoolyard joke! Later she'd check my jeans

For condoms, till I wanted to raise hell.
Oh, how I fucked and fought in adolescence
While she retreated more and more to prayer.
I justified my passion to rebel
By quoting Marx and Lenin, Che Guever-
"Ah! Ah! Ah! That's more the essence,"

You'd say in *Macho Men/Their Mothers*. But hear
The actor wants to take his makeup off!
I hate the ignorance of peasants. Food, more food,
This revolution to deny their fear
That God The Father's dead. Please, don't scoff
At my simplistic use of you. I brood

About my motives when I strategize.
I want to be free. *They* want to be red.
Illiterates and autodidacts, they
Quote me Marx, Lenin, while Communism dies
All over Europe! They want to get ahead,
These bureaucrats-to-be, the proven way.

How can I live with my own fabrication?
How can I live freely, not revolted,
Not a tyrant to myself, not led
Into self-assassination?
Wouldn't Larry, that idealist, be jolted
If he could see the drama in my head,

The sacrificial rite that makes t.v.?
Since Our Father died, we need blood, more blood
—The Kennedys, Martin Luther King.
The final makeup they will do on me
Will simply be my face shoved down in mud,
My brothers and my sisters pummeling.

THE HEADHUNTER

Sorry. Didn't mean to bump into you.
Never thought I'd say that in this five
Bedroom, three bathroom co-op Larry has . . .
"Joe." Your average Joe, trying to survive
Rent, taxes with no deductions. You are who?
A starving member of the middle class
—A shrink! Who doesn't let a minute pass
For free! Am I breaking a taboo
By joking about money? All one's drive

Accomplishes is to put you in reverse.
I am a Headhunter who's forced to work
Eat, screw, and read *The Wall Street Journal* in one
Room smaller than this living room, a jerk
Who even in his thirties was perverse
Enough to think the future would be "fun."
Doesn't it seem that everything you've done
Is worthless, and that everything is worse,
That the I.R.S. Is driving us berserk?

But no one in this country will rebel
On his own behalf. Let the Communist
Chinese peasant chop off his landlord's head.
Don't say you have your own right to resist!
The Boston Tea Party is our parallel,
But we're screwed more. What do we do instead?
We throw a cocktail party for the bed
Of this guy pinching bottoms here pell mell.
Why don't we fight for *our* right to exist?

Twenty years ago I marched for Civil Rights,
Against The War—who cares about the rent!

We masochistically submit and pay
The past, the future to the government.
Forget the present, any big delights
In your one room, driving your Chevrolet,
Your insides eaten up by parasites.
You, not your money, is what winds up spent.

Everyone is listening with smiles. All right,
Then I'll speak up:
                                        It's twenty years ago,
Except the underprivileged is you
And me—the average Jane, the average Joe,
Each friend of Quistador who's here tonight
—Black and white, Catholic, Protestant, Jew,
We're suffering. What are *we* going to do
—Act young and sentimental, underwrite
Coca fields for this sly Mustachio,

Or take our own life with, er in our hands?
A slip, the Doctor smiles. Of course I'm crazy
—From working 9 to 9 for Uncle Sam
Who in the '60s called us "hippies," "lazy."
I'm glad to see that someone understands.
Your nodding, Sir, is welcome. Thank you, Mam.
Maybe I'm loaded. I don't give a damn.
Why don't we learn to make our own demands?
Like Señor Wences here. You're looking hazy

—When we were kids, he was a t.v. puppeteer
Who made a face with lipstick on his hand.
He entertains us now with politics,
Except we liberals fail to understand

The underpinnings of our Help is Fear
—Of Uncle Sammy's cutting off our dicks.
So we're distracted by the Señor's *shticks*.
Before they altogether disappear,
We'll vicariously join his rebel band.

No, Larry, I don't want to stop or leave
Until I'm sober. What I want to do
Is really radicalize this crowd,
Make them uncomfortable—You! You! You!—
By telling them what they deep down believe,
By saying what they only say aloud
In psychotherapy where it's allowed.
Am I right, Doctor? Don't tug my sleeve,
Larry, you *hand*! This really is a coup.

I'm going to sit-in in the dining room,
And anyone who cares to join me, please
Come with me now and make your protest heard
—Above the sipping wine and nibbling cheese—
That we are fed up with the doom and gloom
We live in, hippie babies left in turd,
Too fixed in time to say a single word.
Won't a magical economic boom
Save us? *We* are the Communist Chinese!

MARK STERN

The guy who's sitting in is not an ass.
My wife and I can only have one child
Because today you can't be middle class
And live in New York City and survive
On less than maybe eighty, ninety grand.
The cost of rent and school here drives me wild.
My daughter wants a sister, brother. I've
Tried to explain to her we can't afford
An extra room, a second bill for school,
That public schools are overcrowded, violent,
That she'd be scared there, or at best be bored.
She looks at me as if I am a fool.
Go make a second-grader understand
I spent ten thousand dollars last year just
For school and camp. The consequence? *I'm* cruel.
Go tell that to the U.S. Government
When tax time comes! I work two jobs. My wife
Works one. I know I'm shortening my life
To pay a nanny and a girl to dust.
Crazy. Crazy. Crazy. Why do we stay?
Who would hire a forty-three-year old
Who markets New York City souvenirs?
My wife has tenure at Queens College—gold.
Besides, there is the opera, the ballet,
The theater, restaurants, museums, the stores,
The hi tech energy. Across the street
From us the supermarket stays awake
All night. At 3 A.M. I want some cake,
A hard salami sandwich, eggs and lox.
I put my coat on—and my shoes and socks—
And saunter (unafraid of getting mugged)
To Grand Union or the coffee shop

—The Greek's, who knows I'm sleepless, knows I'm bugged
By money. We commiserate like whores,
Or actors reading that their play's a flop.

When I review the story of my life,
Waiting till thirty-five to have a child,
Till we could learn to live with chronic fear,
Till I could stop bickering with my wife
Because the skimpy future drove us wild . . .
And now she teaches poetry but dreams of money,
And that guy's sitting in to save his soul!
Right on! We're drones and taxes are our honey!
You want to know the hottest souvenir
I sell? A New York City beggar's bowl.
I'm going in to cross my legs and sing
With him, "Oh, we shall overcome someday,"
When rents go down, when they end death and taxes,
When we are not mutated by adapting
—Unable to have the sons we want. I want to say,
The only way it seems you can relax is
To sit in an Eastern position, passive.
These problems both seem petty and feel massive,
And, I'm ashamed to say, just make me numb
To our city's spiritually dying.
I used to call my bourgeois parents "dumb"
And marched, like him, for everybody's rights
But ours. We played at being self-denying
—A comedy—till someone hit the lights!

TO JOYCE

You've done a good job with this party, Joyce.
The food is well-prepared, the guests are chatty
—Especially to me, "The Shrink!" I know
Their conflicts, psychobabble blow by blow.
But I love The Human Comedy: that batty

Renee, that crud dancing with her now,
With that squint, with that confidential voice.
He's out for trouble . . . I won't tell you how.
Unless it happens. Tell me what your son
Is up to lately . . . Goddamnit, Joyce:

On heavy drugs? He's . . . Yes, but not the type
To snort cocaine. God help the middle classes,
Exposed to all the advertising hype
Glamorizing these rock star asses.
Reading Freud's *Cocaine Papers* is no defense.

Freud had his nuttiness: his love for Fleiss
His anger at his Mom displaced to men.
This scotch is strong. I hope I'm making sense . . .
Your son should hear you need a little peace
After your husband's death. Let him take up Zen.

You've done, you'll do the very best you can . . .
What kind of influence will Larry be,
If he decides to take on Marriage, Inc.?
Sorry for joking. I'm your biggest fan.
Larry will fight his own passivity

By sparking Steve to a war of liberation
From drugs, low self-esteem, and hurting you
—Unless his rivalry . . . Dammit, I think
I'm speculating like the starting shrink
I was when you were my best student, who

Flirted with me with that crooked smile,
Brushed my hand lightly when I walked down your aisle,
Who when I'd ramble on like this would wink
To show you weren't nervous—are you?—with this
          conversation . . .
Why did I fight my own infatuation?

If I could tell you, I would tell you how
When I made love to Mary, I would think
Of you, years later even, wondering if that link
Between us still existed; if you'd still allow
Yourself to fantasize about me—when you tried

To make your marriage work, or when your husband died
And Larry baby lay down by your side.
Jesus, I'm getting drunk, forgive me please.
That crooked smile again. I see the plate
Of deli, watch it! wobbling on your knees.

Don't cry, Joyce. Not here, among these strangers
Time passes, what can we do? We make mistakes
That last a lifetime. Maybe it's not too late
To plunge into new combinations, dangers.
Do I still love her? Like a brother. Fate

Turns me to you, slowly, turns you to me,
In spite of all the years since yesterday.
We're cursed by our sensitivity,
You to your husband, me to my wife. It aches
To see you get involved again. It takes

All my resources to watch you with that twerp,
Larry, because that coke-head needs a Dad.
Wow! My emotions are running away
With me, this shrink who's turning gray.
If we don't act right now, we'll both go mad,
If Oedipus refuses to usurp
His superego. I am using this
Psychobabble now, instead of purp-
le language, when I really want to kiss
Your lips like this . . . Who cares what people say?

This is a night for rebels, let's rebel.
Instead of sitting-in, let's sit out Time;
Pretend that once more I am twenty-five
And you're eighteen and wanting to raise hell.
Oh, we have such a drive to stay alive,
Put song to our years-long pantomime
Of finding love and throwing it away
Or, as the poet says, let's seize the day,

Let's take my car and fill it up with gas
And sit like teenagers together, ass to ass
And ride, who cares! tonight to Timbuktu.
I'll call my wife and tell her I love you,
I'll call my service, cancel everyone,
And you'll call Larry, call your mangy son.

And if somebody goes out of his mind . . .
We haven't much time left till we're dead.
Joyce, I'm so tired of living in my head.
Get your bag, and leave your keys behind.
Come, help me dig my coat out of your bed.
It's nearly tomorrow now. It's time we fled.

LARRY'S PLEA

What the hell is going on here, pal of mine?
I get this guy from Quistador, the latest rage
Among our liberati, but these swine
Only rebel against their middle age
—And make me join them in a different way:
I want to run off with Renee, the butcher's honey.
She licks her lips and leads my wits astray.
She talks to me about her clothes, his money,
And I go blank, my blood all in my penis.
She wants to take a ride with me tonight,
And I go get the car keys for this Venus
Without a brain! You understand my plight?
Tell me to stick around for Joyce, my guest,
That all my passion is for politics,
That I'm unique, I'm different from the rest
Of these selfish, adolescent lunatics
Protesting rent and taxes and their death,
That I don't want to reinvent my youth
By taking in Renee's hot, heady breath,
That I'm a moral man who loves the truth,
Not beauty. What will happen to my life
If I give up my values, give up Joyce
And run away to Jersey with *his* wife?
Tell me I have a will, I have a choice,
That she is just my mother in disguise,
That I'm crossing my hands over my cock
Because her looking at me makes it rise,
Puts me in mortal terror of the clock.

She's given me ten minutes to decide,
The whimsical controlling little bitch.
She is the mob, taking me for a ride.

But I am going crazy with this itch!
Tell Joyce, my guest of honor—Honor!—I
Am fighting for my life and had to run,
That I am just an ordinary guy
Who wants the Prom Queen, wants to be twenty-one.
This dread is contagious. What about you?
You're my age, Ben. Stop me from what I'm going to do.

RENEE

I know you're Larry's confidant,
And maybe Joyce's lover. No?
Not till Larry and I split!
He hasn't talked about this? Oh,
I hope he doesn't have a fit
About what girls can say or can't.

Well, anyway, my husband spoke
About our marriage, which I'm sure
You see is just a joke.
You don't? Didn't he say he's limp
And thinks that I'm a slut, impure
For wanting sex? That oaf, that wimp.

That King of everybody's meat
But his—that's why he acts macho,
Wrecking furniture when I cheat.
Big man, grabbing a chair or table,
Or going on t.v. as "Meato,"
The hairy star of late night cable.

In college I was never shy.
Would you be if you had the looks?
I wanted Larry even then,
But he was always buried in his books.
I always slept with lesser men
Because they had the guts to try

For what they thought they couldn't get,
Like Meato with his low I.Q.
Powering for a million bucks
And getting it—instead of you,
Your soul so compassionate it's wet.
As Meato says in bed, "Life sucks."

Money has given Larry guts
To entertain like this, act debonair,
Joke, "Renee baby, be my bimbo."
And when I challenge, "Part my hair,"
He doesn't give me "buts"
About leaving Joyce in limbo

But kicks his bedroom door shut and
Clicks my car keys in his open hand
And sweeps me tango-like to kiss
And tells me I'm no "Mom" or "Sis."
What, I wonder, did he mean by that?
Anyway, it's nice to stand and chat

But Larry's holding up ten
Fingers meaning, *Say goodnight to Ben,*
And tell him please take care of Joyce.
Larry's leaving you no other choice.
And if my Meato starts to wreck this place,
Please tell him that he's suffering disgrace,
And that he's breaking Larry's coffee cup,
Because he couldn't get his own meat up.

JOYCE'S SON

Doe, ain't it sickening, these fat cats wailing
About their rent and taxes, when Quistadorians die
                    in the hills?
What did they come here for? What kind of thrills
Did they expect from these brave men
Who seem to be prevailing

Over a tyrant who'd knock out teeth for gold?
And they come from the '60s
—Ex-hippies, radicals, SNCC or some weird *shtick* . . .
Does middle age make everybody sick?
They've done some spiritual striptease,
Then panicked at the thought of getting old

And covered themselves with polyester, jewels
Like Tim Leary, Jerry Rubin—the epitome
Of them all, Yuppies once Yippies—fools,
Shutup in there, I can't stand your hypocrisy!

You see that guy? He's the right hand
Of our Guest of Honor, even stronger,
An idealist who doesn't understand
Why his leader stays here a second longer.

He wants me to go to Quistador
And help raise money, smuggling drugs
Instead of sitting cross-legged on this floor
And singing, "We shall overcome" with bourgeoise thugs.

I tell you this because I can't tell Joyce
Face to face. She'll think, and maybe say
In her hysterically calmest voice,
I'll go because—she has to know!—I'm gay.

I tell you this, not Larry, not because
He's an asshole, shallow, narcissistic,
But because Mom will need you through this loss.
She loves you, Doctor, let's be realistic,

More than she ever loved my Dad or me.
It hurts, but I'm no '60s Pollyanna.
I won't grow into fat hypocrisy.
I'm taking to the hills in a read bandanna.

• • •

Mom, what are you doing with that suitcase? Doc?
I don't believe this fantasy is true!
No, this is great. Who wanted you to marry
That Sissypuss, that Larry?
I'm glad the Doc is taking up with you,
As I am taking up with that great cock.

Why the hell did I say that,
Like some loony blurting dirty words?
Where's Larry going with Renee?
It looks like they're also running away,
While Meato's sitting-in with those gilt turds.
Okay, I'll tell you, Mom, exactly where I'm at . . .

THE GUEST OF HONOR TALKS
ABOUT JOYCE'S SON

He's wrong. This sit-in, selfish as it seems,
Is how a real revolt must actually start,
Not with the head, some theoretician's dreams,
But with the growling belly and the heart.

Who's the first to die in any revolution?
Not the salesman or the meat inspector,
Or the maker of the previous Constitution,
But the gouging landlord and the tax collector.

Of course I find them irritating, worse,
They'd be the ruling class in Quistador,
Discourteous and morally perverse,
Sitting and chanting on the marble floor

"Yankee Go Home? No, You Go Home, Juarez!"
Yet who is more absurd: those fools or me?
Or Napoleon's troops singing the Marseillaise?
Or you Colonists revolting over tea?

My cynicism seems a muddle now,
Lacking in wit, not sharp, I'm getting drunk.
I ought to leave before I start a row
And lose the money of this Yankee punk

With which I'll keep my life a little longer,
Before some monomaniac, well-fed
Because of Hotsupr's efforts, and far stronger
Ideologically, shoots me dead.

But you're distracted, I'm a bore.
My problems, after hours, can't be fun.
God, I feel dizzy. Is it hot here, or . . . ?
Why did that woman slap her son?

Is my comrade grinning at them or at me?
I have to sit down. Shit. Doctor, I think
With all my talk, the actuality
Is: my right hand put something in my drink . . .

Doctor, I think—my throat is dry—he'll blame
My death on Yankees, martyr me to feed
—Food, food!—The Cause. Enjoy my fame,
My false ideals, Jimenez! Doctor, I need . . .

JOYCE'S PLEA

Why is Juarez collapsed?
Stop that singing! What?
Ben, bang on his chest!

Steve, get the cops, the Guest
Is dying. Or lapsed
Into a coma. Is this a plot

To assassinate him? Steve,
Where are you going?
Cutting the phone lines—why? . . .
No, it's not true. Lie.
This is no time to leave,
You'll look guilty. Stop that singing!

• • •

I don't know where your Renee has gone.
Yes, she left with Larry. Stop
Throwing furniture, "Meato!"
This is some revolution. Go
Down to the doorman and get a cop.

• • •

All revolution's a farce, a piling on
Of one betrayal, then another.
As the body revolts in middle age
Or passion burdens a burdened life,
Or a man suddenly dies on his wife,
Or a wife leaves him struggling with rage,
Or a son, in an instant, destroys his mother.

• • •

Ben, you have our hero breathing hard!
Let's help him to the shower, Meato.
Forget your wife, be altruistic.
So what if he is "communistic."
Doctor, you are magnifico:
Out hero's throwing up, thank God,

And they're still singing,
Though the world's turned upside down.
I think it's the cops, the doorbell's ringing.
Let's open it, and then get out of town.

THE PSYCHIATRIST'S EPILOGUE

I'm getting tipsy, Joyce, but I want to make
A toast before the dawn, before we wake
Into a real awareness of the chaos here,
And either call it ours, or disappear.
I've seen it always and I've seen it all
—No difference between the tragic and the comic fall,
Except in one the clowns get up to play
Only to drop dead on another day
Because of some slight quirk, some accident
While protesting the taxes or the rent.
So while we're only middle-aged, my friends,
Keep spending time unmindful that it ends.
Down in the streets the sun is coming up.
I toast it with the whiskey in this cup.
In spite of our intentions, curses, hopes,
Life has its way with us—the geniuses and dopes.
No matter what religion we profess
—Therapy, politics—we can only guess
Our fates, and then they prove us wrong. The wheel
Of Fortune must hand us a dirty deal.
But in the meantime, let's watch the dust appear
To dance in the sunlight, as I'm standing here,
As last night, another life ago,
We swore that we'd be young and simply go.
But now that seems a gesture we have to make,
Therapeutic, for our soul's or psyche's sake.
You feel the same—to leave or not to leave,
To rock and roll the moment that we grieve,
Or else to find your son and me my wife,
Return to an irrevocably altered life.
What shall we do? says The Mentor to his Joyce:
Be old or young again? What's your choice?

BIOGRAPHICAL NOTE

Frederick Feirstein has had nine previous books of poems published, seven by Story Line and the Quarterly Review of Literature. He has been the recipient of a Guggenheim Fellowship, the Poetry Society of America's John Masefield Award, and England's Arvon Prize. Twelve of his plays have been produced. Three are musical dramas, his lyrics deriving from his poetry. His third, *Uprising*, will be done as a film. He made his living writing film and television while he trained as a psychoanalyst. He is in private practice in New York City and on the faculty of the National Psychological Association for Psychoanalysis. His autobiography is in the Contemporary Authors Autobiography Series and his biography in the Dictionary of Literary Biography.